D1014183

Paws for a moment with God

Devotions *Best Enjoyed in the Company of a Cat*

Paws for a Moment with God
©Product Concept Mfg., Inc.

Paws for a Moment with God
ISBN 978-0-9843328-8-5

Published by Product Concept Mfg., Inc.
2175 N. Academy Circle #200, Colorado Springs, CO 80909

©2010 Product Concept Mfg., Inc. All rights reserved.

All scripture quotations are from the King James version
of the Bible unless otherwise noted.

Scriptures taken from the Holy Bible,
New International Version®, NIV®.
Copyright © 1973, 1978, 1984 by Biblica, Inc.™
Used by permission of Zondervan.
All rights reserved worldwide.
www.zondervan.com

Sayings not having a credit listed are contributed by writers
for Product Concept Mfg., Inc. or in a rare case,
the author is unknown.

Written and Compiled by Patricia Mitchell
in association with Product Concept Mfg., Inc.

All Rights Reserved. Except for brief quotes used in
reviews, articles, or other media, no part of this book
may be reproduced or transmitted in any form or by
any means, electronic or mechanical, including
photocopying, recording, or by information or
retrieval system, without permission by the publisher.

Paws for a moment with God

God must have been smiling when He created the cat! He made them in sizes, shapes, and colors designed to please their human companions, and He gave them soft fur and melodic purrs guaranteed to bring them close to our hearts.

Cats can be funny and reserved, content and curious, shy and affectionate, scrappy and serene – sometimes all in one day! They also can teach us some of life's most important truths and spiritual lessons just by being who they are... our feline friends and gentle companions, a purrfect blessing from heaven.

May this little book of reflections, famous quotations, and classic and contemporary poems make you smile as you read Bible-centered devotions, each one drawn from the attitude, antics, and presence of our beloved cats.

Without a sound,

the gray striped cat

saunters to the ribbon of sunlight

streaming into the room.

She stops, her head held high,

and sniffs the afternoon air.

Satisfied, she reclines,

stretching herself long and thin

in the warming ray,

wearing the unmistakable

look of pure bliss.

Life's Freebies

Have you ever noticed how a cat will find contentment in something as simple as a ray of sunshine? She settles herself in its pleasure and basks in the joy of the moment!

Every day, God sends simple blessings into our lives for us to discover, embrace, and enjoy. A cooling breeze on a hot summer's day. A toasty fire on a chilly afternoon. The song of leaves rustling in the wind. The sound of birds chirping from the rooftop.

God's simple blessings come completely free—it's just a matter of taking the time to enjoy them.

This is the day which the LORD hath made;
we will rejoice and be glad in it.
Psalm 118:24

From another room comes the sound

of jingle bells and ping pong balls,

of fuzzy mice tossed into the air

and catnip sacks chased until

they disappear under the sofa.

In cat years, he's not a kitten anymore

. . . but he hasn't forgotten how to play!

Simple Pleasures

The calendar fills up quickly, and we rush from one place to the next, from one task to another. It's no wonder we're exhausted at the end of the day!

No matter how distant our childhood years, a little time out each day for play can work wonders. It relieves physical and mental stress, and helps keep life in balance. It provides a new perspective on the tasks at hand, and lets us return to the serious stuff renewed and refreshed.

Most important, it reminds us that God loves to hear His children of all ages at play.

Rejoice evermore.
1 Thessalonians 5:16

When I play with my cat,
who knows if I am not a pastime to her
more than she is to me?

Michel de Montaigne

You will always be lucky if you know
how to make friends with strange cats.

American Proverb

A cat's eyes are windows
enabling us to see into another world.
Irish Legend

If animals could speak,
the dog would be a blundering outspoken fellow;
but the cat would have the rare grace
of never saying a word too much.
Mark Twain

A cat pours his body on the floor like water.
It is restful just to see him.
William Lyon Phelps

There is little that annoys a cat more than a closed door. She will howl, scratch, and paw at the door until it is opened. Then, immediately, her anxiety fades like a whisper, and she enters with queenly dignity. Finding the space insufferably dull, she exits with not a single look back.

A Good Place

We counted on that promotion, but didn't get it. We put our hopes and dreams into a relationship, but it didn't work out. We longed to join in the fun, but couldn't.

It's true: sometimes God says No. Despite our pleading, God keeps a door shut when He knows what's behind it isn't the right place for us to be. It is in these times that He invites us to look around, because there's a door waiting for our knock—a door He will open and a place He will give us as our own.

Ask, and it shall be given you;
seek, and ye shall find; knock,
and it shall be opened unto you.
Matthew 7:7

Little kitty, where did you come from?

What is your name?

Leaves and twigs hang from your coat,

and your cries tell of hunger and chill.

Come, come!

There's fresh milk for your belly,

a warm lap for your chill,

a cozy room for your shelter,

and most of all, a friend who loves you.

A Friend in Him

Most of us know what it feels like to enter a crowded room and recognize no one there. With what relief we hear a familiar voice break through the noise and see a good friend happily heading in our direction!

Jesus came to Earth to be that good Friend for us. When we think we're lost in the world, He comforts us with His presence. When we feel like strangers in a foreign land, He calls us by name and reminds us of His love. No matter where we are, we have a Friend in Him.

The LORD is my shepherd; I shall not want.
Psalm 23:1

The Kitten and the Falling Leaves

See the kitten on the wall,
Sporting with the leaves that fall,
Withered leaves - one - two - three -
From the lofty elder-tree! . . .
And I will have my careless season
Spite of melancholy reason,
Will walk through life in such a way
That, when time brings on decay,
Now and then I may possess
Hours of perfect gladsomeness.

–Pleased by any random toy;
By a kitten's busy joy,
Or an infant's laughing eye
Sharing in the ecstasy;
I would fare like that or this,
Find my wisdom in my bliss;
Keep the sprightly soul awake,
And have faculties to take,
Even from things by sorrow wrought,
Matter for a jocund thought,
Spite of care, and spite of grief,
To gambol with Life's falling Leaf.

William Wordsworth (excerpt)

The Siamese cat saunters past the large brown dog, seemingly without a care in the world. Doesn't she realize how big that dog is? Shouldn't she cower in fear? No, not at all. The Siamese cat holds her head high and claims her place in the world with quiet confidence.

Lion Hearted

Big problems can make us feel small, afraid, and ineffective. The thought of confronting a hard truth or standing up to a difficult person can fill anyone's heart with misgivings. We would rather simply skirt the problem than meet it head-on!

In His goodness, God assures us that we need never face life's challenges alone. He sends us His Spirit to remind us of His presence and to give us the confidence we need to handle life's biggest, toughest, and scariest obstacles. (And sometimes, it's our God-given courage that cuts those problems down to size!)

The wicked flee when no man pursueth:
but the righteous are bold as a lion.
Proverbs 28:1

The ancient tom settles on the

window seat for his morning's

pleasure. Though he no longer

yearns and clamors to hurry

outside and scamper through the

blossoms, he watches the world

through the perceptive eyes

of years . . .

and the contented smile

of sweet remembering.

It seems at every life stage, we're immersed in things to do. We have schoolwork and jobs inside and outside the home. We take up sports and hobbies, interests and activities. As we grow older, however, many of us find ourselves not quite up to doing all we used to do.

A slower lifestyle is a blessing when it brings us closer to things that really matter – to reflection on God's promises and His truth, to prayer for ourselves and for others, to gratitude for His work in our lives and in our world.

Though time may take away, God gives in abundance to those who look to Him.

Even to your old age and gray hairs I am he,
I am he who will sustain you.
Isaiah 46:4 NIV

They say the test of literary power
is whether a man can write an inscription.
I say, "Can he name a kitten?"

Samuel Butler

There is nothing sweeter than his peace
when at rest. For there is nothing
brisker than his life when in motion.

Christopher Smart

Animals are such agreeable friends -
they ask no questions, they pass no criticisms.

George Eliot

The matronly calico knows when someone's missing. Yes, one of us is away for a few days and will return tomorrow. But the calico will sit tonight at the top of the stairs, attentive for the sounds of a car motor, a turning lock, and a familiar voice calling her name.

Home Again

While a vacation offers a change of pace and the chance to see new places, coming home is a pleasure all its own. It's comforting to find ourselves back in familiar surroundings once again.

Though we often stray from God, He waits patiently for us to return home to Him. No matter how far we might have gone, God's mercy and forgiveness respond to the sound of our confession and the sincerity of our repentance.

When we wander away from our spiritual home in Him, we are welcome back at any time. He waits for us with open arms.

Joy shall be in heaven over one sinner that repenteth, more than over ninety and nine just persons, which need no repentance.
Luke 15:7

Before she sleeps, the little white cat takes her nightly bath. She wipes her face with her paw, then bends to lick belly and back, her legs and tail. When all has been completed to her satisfaction, she stretches, then curls herself comfortably, closing her eyes with a low, contented purr.

One of the many blessings God gives those who trust in Him is the gift of a good night's sleep.

When we release the day's worries and troubles into His hands, we are free to sleep in peace. We know our God is in control, and our nights hold no terror for us, nor will we spend its precious hours fretting over what might happen tomorrow.

As someone once said, "When you can't sleep, don't count sheep, but talk to the Shepherd." A good night's sleep brings the physical and spiritual refreshment God intends for His people.

It is vain for you to rise up early, to sit up late,
to eat the bread of sorrows:
for so he giveth his beloved sleep.
Psalm 127:2

Cat Facts

Though cats do not live in packs like dogs, a cat is a social being. Cat companions have long known that their feline friends respond to speech, take pleasure in human company, and are aware of the comings and goings of the household.

When a cat is happy, she holds her tail upright, but when anxious or nervous, she drags her tail behind her. A slowly swishing tail means she is investigating something, while a rapidly swishing tail means she is irritated. When a cat fluffs out her tail, she is reacting to fear – she hopes to scare off a predator by appearing larger than she is.

Another way to gauge a cat's mood is to look into his eyes. Though a cat's pupils will narrow in bright sunlight and widen as light diminishes, his pupils also will narrow if he is angry or irritated. An excited or playful cat will have large, round pupils.

While many cats prefer living as the only cat on the premises, they can live happily in multi-cat households. Introduce new members slowly, giving all cats a chance to get to know one another in safe conditions and under supervision. Give special attention to the resident cats so they know they are being neither replaced nor ignored. The home should provide enough room for each cat to stake out his own territory. Make sure plenty of food (in separate dishes) is readily available, and set out a litter box for each cat, plus an extra box. With space, time, and love, happy families are born!

You know, don't you?
Your human companion doesn't
feel well today, so you spend time by
her side instead of watching birds
or chasing your favorite toy mouse.
You nuzzle her gently, you lick her
hand tenderly, and you settle on the
pillow next to hers, keeping watch
with sympathetic eyes.

His Promise

Sometimes all it takes is an encouraging word or a listening ear to let someone know we care. A few moments of our time and our genuine interest can go a long way toward helping a friend through a tough situation, or supporting a loved one in difficult circumstance.

Our presence for others reflects God's presence in our lives. No, He's not always going to provide an instant solution to our problems, and He may not necessarily offer a miracle cure, but He has promised to be there to help us though. We can depend on Him.

My spirit remaineth
among you: fear ye not.
Haggai 2:5

Silly kitty, dashing back and forth from room to room! Are you chasing ghosts? Are you racing with the shadows on the wall? You leave the rugs in a heap behind you as you slide around corners, then you suddenly stop the game and settle sedately in your favorite chair.

Ha, Ha, Ha!

"Laughter is the best medicine." It's true! Laughter relieves stress, lifts the spirit, and enhances our ability to meet life's challenges. A good laugh relaxes muscles, releases beneficial chemicals into the body, strengthens the immune system, and increases blood flow, which can help prevent cardiovascular problems. Simply put, laughter makes us feel good all over – and what's more, it's free!

The joy and pleasure of laughter is a gift God desires us to use, and use liberally, every day. There's only one thing better than a good laugh, and that's a good laugh shared with those around us!

My mouth shall praise thee with joyful lips.
Psalm 63:5

The Cat and the Moon

The cat went here and there
and the moon spun round like a top,
and the nearest kin of the moon,
the creeping cat, looked up.
Black Minnaloushe stared at the moon,
for, wander and wail as he would,
the pure cold light in the sky
troubled his animal blood. . . .

Minnaloushe runs in the grass
Lifting his delicate feet.
Do you dance, Minnaloushe, do you dance?
When two close kindred meet,
what better than call a dance?

–William Butler Yeats (excerpt)

Nothing escapes the notice of the tortoiseshell cat. As she walks, her head turns side to side as she tries not to miss any interesting thing that might appear in the room she left only an hour ago. Now what's this? It could be a speck of dust, a thread, or a sunbeam that draws her undivided attention.

Wonders Waiting

God created a world of wonders, and we don't need to go far from home to see them. Why? Because His wonders are all around us, no matter where we live!

As we go about the business of our day, it's easy to pass by the simple delight of a flower blooming, a robin singing, a child giggling. In an effort to get everything on our to-do list finished, we forget to look down at the grass and look up at the stars. All too often, we even neglect to look at each other!

Discovering new things is not about going someplace else, but in looking here with attentive eyes.

And thou shalt rejoice in every good thing
which the LORD thy God hath given unto thee,
and unto thine house...
Deuteronomy 26:11

"Pay attention to me!"

chatters the calico cat when she

sees the tiger tom on my lap.

Sometimes she'll nudge the tom off

and quickly take his place.

Other times she'll turn with

a grumbling meow and perch

herself on the book shelf where

she watches the goings-on with

disapproving eyes.

Rejoice

How must our petty jealousies and trivial annoyances look to our Heavenly Father, who loves each of us with an overwhelming love?

God sends His Holy Spirit into our hearts to help us let go of human frailties that keep us from genuine affection, acceptance, and contentment. The Holy Spirit reminds us of God's overwhelming love for us, and opens our hearts to God-like love for others.

In Him, we have the power to rejoice in the good fortune of others and to embrace all the goodness and mercy He has in store for us.

Let us not love in word, neither in tongue;
but in deed and in truth.
1 John 3:18

Cat Quotes

The smallest feline is a masterpiece.

Leonardo da Vinci

Cat's motto: No matter what you've done wrong, always try to make it look like the dog did it.

Author Unknown

You don't truly understand rejection
until you have been ignored by a cat.

Author Unknown

In a cat's eye, all things belong to cats.

English Proverb

Dogs have owners, but cats have staff.

Author Unknown

The feisty gray cat moves

with a swagger, daring all comers

to beat him in a match of wits and claws.

He spies the tuxedo cat dozing by

a window. The gray cat glares.

The tuxedo opens his eyes,

and in one flawless movement,

glides off his chair and disappears.

God at Work

"An eye for an eye" our thinking goes. A person has provoked us by speaking out of turn, and we respond in kind. But what would have happened if we responded not with words, but simply by walking away?

A heart of forgiveness takes no offense at the petty provocations of others, nor does it see fit to retaliate in kind. A heart of forgiveness never follows where God's Spirit would not take it, but leads by loving example.

Our refusal to take personal offense and our willingness to forgive others reveals God at work in our lives.

Make sure that nobody
pays back wrong for wrong,
but always try to be kind
to each other and to everyone else.
1 Thessalonians 5:15 NIV

Kitties, kitties all around! Of course, it's dinner time, and they circle the kitchen with impatient meows and nudges and leg rubs while bowls are set out and cans are opened. Once the meal is served, each cat, without further ado, laps up her generous portion.

The Source

God sends blessings to all, believers and non-believers alike. His warming sun shines and His soft showers fall on the lands of the godly and the ungodly... of all who live on Earth.

The difference lies not in the blessings God sends, but in how people respond to them. While non-believers receive His many blessings, they do not know whom to thank for their good fortune.

To believing hearts only comes the God-given ability to know who preserves and blesses the Earth. To Him we offer our gratitude and praise for all we receive from His hand.

He maketh his sun to rise on the evil and on the good, and sendeth rain on the just and on the unjust.
Matthew 5:45

A cat came fiddling out of a barn
with a pair of bag-pipes under her arm.
She could sing nothing but Fiddle dee dee,
the mouse has married the bumble-bee.
Pipe, cat; dance, mouse -
we'll have a wedding at our good house.

Traditional Rhyme

There Was a Crooked Man

There was a crooked man

and he walked a crooked mile,

He found a crooked sixpence

upon a crooked stile.

He bought a crooked cat,

which caught a crooked mouse,

And they all lived together

in a little crooked house.

Traditional Rhyme

The black and white cat stretches in a ray of sunshine, basking in the warming rays, rolling in the soft springtime grass. Her eyelids close lightly, for she rests at ease, yet still alert for the rustle of leaves and the first scent of danger in the wind.

Creativity

Ah, for the ease a lazy afternoon can bring! Though we may feel guilty for "doing nothing" when we have so much on our calendar, carefree hours are necessary for our spiritual health and well-being.

Without giving ourselves time out, we miss the simple pleasure of being... just living, breathing, thinking in God's good creation. We're opening ourselves to wherever our thoughts, dreams, and imagination may lead us. During times of rest and relaxation, we're allowing ourselves to hear the whisper of our inmost being... the voice of our creative soul.

Bless the LORD, O my soul:
and all that is within me, bless his holy name.
Psalm 103:1

Look at the little white kitten, her head brushed with a smattering of gold and her tail kissed with sunshine! She sits in quiet contentment, a circle of serenity, barely moving a muscle, her paws together as if it is her time for meditative prayer.

Paws for Prayer

Our Heavenly Father invites us to come to Him in prayer. What a unique privilege we have been given!

Prayer is our opportunity to talk to God about anything that burdens our heart, whether our own troubles or the troubles of a friend or loved one. Doesn't God know about these things? Of course He does, but He desires to hear us tell Him in our own words, and then give over the problem to Him.

Contact God, who already has contacted you with His love. Take Him up on His invitation to pray. Your Heavenly Father listens, and He cares.

Blessed be the LORD, because he hath heard
the voice of my supplications.
Psalm 28:6

A Cat Companion's Prayer

Because I'm only human,
it's sometimes hard to be
The wise, all-knowing creature
that my cat expects of me.
And so I pray for special help
to somehow understand

The subtle implications of
each proud meowed command.
I know it's really lots to ask,
but please, oh please, take pity;
Although I'm only human,
make me worthy of my kitty!

Author Unknown

Pretty kitty! You're used to hearing those words, aren't you? Without a whiff of embarrassment or a blush of discomfort, you draw near for more sweet praises, for long strokes on your silky coat, for a cuddle, perhaps, and more compliments on your supreme and thoroughly wondrous splendor.

Thank You!

Perhaps there is no such thing as even a minimally humble cat, but there are many extraordinarily humble Christians. Some are so "humble" that they allow no praise for anything they do!

Exaggerated humility prevents others from recognizing the gifts God has given us. By contrast, gracious humility accepts earned compliments, always giving the glory to God, because it is in Him we have our power and strength.

While at times we may want to remain the anonymous angel, there also are times we may accept acknowledgement of God's work in our lives. A heartfelt "thank you" marks genuine humility.

Whether therefore ye eat, or drink,
or whatsoever ye do, do all to the glory of God.
1 Corinthians 10:31

It's true, little one . . .

you're not an elegant cat.

Your fur looks tousled and

rumpled no matter how often

you're brushed, or how long

you spend at your toilette.

But who cares? You don't.

You go on being the sweetest

and friendliest of all kitties,

and clearly, you possess a

very elegant heart.

Hey, Good Looking!

As good stewards of the body God has given us, we strive to present a positive image to others. Yet there's something far more important than what we look like on the outside, and that's who we are on the inside.

Inner qualities such as character, integrity, honesty, kindness, and genuine love for others far outweigh mere physical charm. In the heart is where God looks, and in the heart is where true beauty lies. And here's good news for those of us getting on in years – though outer beauty fades, inner beauty grows only more lustrous with time!

Man looks at the outward appearance,
but the LORD looks at the heart.
1 Samuel 16:7 NIV

To A Cat

Stately, kindly, lordly friend
Condescend
Here to sit by me, and turn
Glorious eyes that smile and burn,
Golden eyes, love's lustrous meed,
On the golden page I read.

All your wondrous wealth of hair,
Dark and fair,
Silken-shaggy, soft and bright
As the clouds and beams of night,
Pays my reverent hand's caress
Back with friendlier gentleness.

–A. C. Swinburne

The gray striped tabby hides upstairs when furniture is moved, for she's a timid and fearful cat. She desires nothing new to confuse her view of the world around her. The gray striped tabby prefers the familiarity and safety of things left just as they are, especially her favorite chair.

Change and More Change

At times, change comes as an unwelcome guest, throwing our plans and expectations into complete chaos. It's tempting to toss our hands in the air and give up.

For believers, however, change takes on a different aspect. No matter how unwanted or unexpected the event, we remember that God remains in control. At all times, we rely on Him to see us through, and we take courage in knowing God has a purpose for all the events of our lives.

We will see and experience change as long as we live here on Earth. What comfort to know our unchangeable God!

Jesus Christ the same yesterday,
and to day, and for ever.
Hebrews 13:8

How tall I must look to you, little kitty! How I tower over you, and yet you're not afraid. You know my hands are gentle and my voice is full of praises for you. You have felt my arms around you, and you doze on my lap, protected, secure, and safe.

Come!

Our God is many things: all-knowing, all-powerful, all-seeing. Yes, He is all of these, yet He invites us to know Him as a compassionate, loving Father. He opens His arms to us, drawing us closer to Him with words of caring and encouragement, understanding and love.

Far from staying far above us, God comes into our lives when we open our heart to Him. He desires to bless us with His presence and help us live more meaningfully, more purposefully, more joyfully.

"Never hesitate," He says. "I am here for you. Do not be afraid. Come!"

Let us therefore come boldly unto the throne of grace,
that we may obtain mercy,
and find grace to help in time of need.
Hebrews 4:16

Belling the Cat

Long ago, the mice held a general council to consider what measures they could take to outwit their common enemy, the Cat. Some said this, and some said that; but at last a young mouse got up and said he had a proposal to make, which he thought would meet the case.

"You will all agree," said he, "that our chief danger consists in the sly and treacherous manner in which the enemy approaches us. Now, if we could receive some signal of her approach, we could easily escape from her. I venture, therefore, to propose that a small bell be procured, and attached by a ribbon round the neck of the Cat. By this means we should always know when she was about, and could easily retire while she was in the neighborhood."

This proposal met with general applause, until an old mouse got up and said, "That is all very well, but who is to bell the Cat?"

The mice looked at one another and nobody spoke. Then the old mouse said, "It is easy to propose impossible remedies."

–Aesop

People come and go on their daily errands. So much to do! So much to clean, fix, buy, set up, and take down! All the while, the fluffy white cat sleeps the afternoon away, content with a full belly, a ray of sunshine, and the sweetness of home and family.

Travel Light

"Travel light" isn't only a way to save on baggage handling fees, but wise advice for daily living.

When we develop the discipline to live within our means, curb our desire for excess material possessions, and avoid overindulgence, we put ourselves in a position to truly enjoy life. We're released from the burden of debt, from the never-ending responsibility of upkeep and storage, and the urge to buy the latest, the newest, and the most impressive.

The Spirit-given gift of contentment with what we have frees us to "travel light" throughout life's journey.

Godliness with contentment is great gain.
1 Timothy 6:6

"No, no, kitty!"

Threads hang from the sofa where

kitty's claws have been.

Though multiple scratching posts

are placed around the house,

kitty prefers to do her work where

she shouldn't. "No, no, kitty!"

She dashes away, only to slink back

into the room and resume her

unfinished business.

Yes, Yes

From our first parents in the Garden of Eden to today, people gravitate toward forbidden fruit. The temptation to do what we know we shouldn't can overwhelm us!

Stained by our sin, we're incompatible with God's pure holiness. Is anyone "good enough" to stand before God? No, no! That's why Jesus, God's Son, took responsibility for our disobedience. He took the cross to spare us our punishment, and He rose again to give us His life.

Because of Jesus, we can repent and ask for forgiveness, never doubting God's willingness and desire to answer "yes, yes" to our heartfelt prayer.

Blessed is he whose transgression is forgiven,
whose sin is covered.
Psalm 32:1

Five Little Eyes

In Hans' old mill his three black cats
watch his bins for the thieving rats.
Whisker and claw, they crouch in the night,
their five eyes smoldering green and bright.
Squeaks from the flour sacks, squeaks from where.
The cold wind stirs on the empty stair,
squeaking and scampering, everywhere.

Then down they pounce, now in, now out,
at whisking tail, and sniffing snout.
While lean old Hans he snores away,
till peep of light at break of day.
Then up he climbs to his creaking mill,
out come his cats all grey with meal.
Jekkel, and Jessup, and one-eyed Jill.

–Walter de la Mare

A comfortable lap,

a gentle stroke, a hand to rub

your outstretched chin . . .

is this kitty paradise?

Your purr-motor's running

passionately, and your paws

are kneading with kittenish zeal

as you close your eyes to all else,

savoring this moment of absolute joy.

Heartfelt Joy

It has been said that Christians are the only people who have good reason to live joyfully. After all, as Christians we possess faith planted by the Holy Spirit; we rely on God's forgiveness through Jesus Christ; and we're assured of God's goodwill and mercy toward us now and forever.

Though life's set-backs, ills, and challenges may cause us temporary unhappiness, the Holy Spirit reminds of God's constant care and ever-present love. This is where true joy comes from – the kind of heart-centered joy in Christ that trials and troubles cannot take away.

The fruit of the Spirit is love, joy, peace, longsuffering, gentleness, goodness, faith, meekness, temperance.
Galatians 5:22-23

A cat with a black satin coat
came to the door, looking up with
pleading eyes. A bowl of food?
A dish of water, please?
Perhaps a place by the fire on such
a chilly, shivery night? Of course.
You've arrived at the right place.
Come in, come in.

The Knock

We stand on the doorstep and knock on the door, expecting to hear familiar footsteps, the click of a lock, and then see the door open and the smiling face of our friend.

Similarly, Jesus stands outside the door of our heart, and He knocks. Then He knocks again. Silence. Our Friend has come to visit, but we are too busy to open the door.

Our Lord continues to knock because He yearns to hear our footsteps, and then the click of a lock. His face breaks into a smile when the door opens and He sees His beloved son... His beloved daughter... welcoming Him inside.

I stand at the door, and knock: if any man hear my voice, and open the door, I will come in to him.
Revelation 3:20

It is a difficult matter to gain the affection of a cat. He is a philosophical, methodical animal, tenacious of his own habits, fond of order and neatness, and disinclined to extravagant sentiment. He will be your friend, if he finds you worthy of friendship, but not your slave.

–Théophile Gautier

A kitten is the delight of a household. All day long a comedy is played by this incomparable actor.

Champfleury

The last thing I would accuse a cat of is innocence.

Edward Paley

What greater gift than the love of a cat?

Charles Dickens

Without a sound,

the cat of the house slips from room to

room on her morning stroll,

peering here and there as she will.

Only when she settles might

she suggest her presence with

a slight meow or a satisfied yawn,

and once she has been noticed,

she closes her eyes for a nap.

Soft Paws

A gentle, unassuming walk through our days and years may not bring us fame, but it has a way of nurturing spiritual growth.

Lack of pretense keeps us in touch with who we are, and frees us to respond to others without regard for what they can do for us. When we're not looking for opportunities to sell ourselves, we're more open to giving what people need most – our love, our care, and our presence.

Gentle footsteps may not be heard around the world, but they will be heard in the hearts of those who mean the most to us.

If a man think himself to be something,
when he is nothing,
he deceiveth himself.
Galatians 6:3

"Why are you pouring coffee for yourself when it's a plate of chopped chicken and gravy I want?"

"I am here at the door, so why don't you get up from your chair and open it for me? Why, oh why?"

As anyone knows,

a cat does not like to wait!

Patience!

For many of us, patience does not come easily. When we set our sights on something, we want it right away!

Many of the best things in life, however, demand – and deserve –patience. To reach a worthy goal or cherished dream, we need time to develop our talent or master a skill. Patience with ourselves and with others brings fulfillment in a way no hasty solution can.

Our spiritual life, too, requires patience. The Holy Spirit works as we study and meditate on God's Word, allowing His biblical truths to permeate our heart as we grow in wisdom and understanding.

I wait for the Lord, my soul doth wait,
and in his word do I hope.
Psalm 130:5

The Owl and the Pussy Cat

The Owl and the Pussy-cat went to sea
In a beautiful pea-green boat.
They took some honey, and plenty of money,
Wrapped up in a five-pound note.

The Owl looked up to the stars above,
And sang to a small guitar,
"O lovely Pussy! O Pussy, my love,
What a beautiful Pussy you are,
You are,
You are!
What a beautiful Pussy you are!"

–Edward Lear

Tufts of fur scoot across the floor and a toy mouse lies in the hallway. Cat scratches stripe a chair, there's a throw over the sofa, and glass figurines sit behind cabinet doors. This house is not chic, but it's something much better - the home of an elegant cat.

Just Right

God would have us give everything we do our best effort, but we will never reach perfection as long as we live in this world. Our Heavenly Father, who is perfect, knows our weaknesses and failings, and certainly our sincere desire to make progress toward the spiritual ideal of perfection pleases Him. But guess what? Though we repeatedly fall short, God looks upon our efforts as perfect because His Son, Jesus Christ, lived the perfect life on our behalf!

Because of Him, we continue to strive, yet we know when to let go. God alone is perfect.

Be ye therefore perfect,
even as your Father which is in heaven is perfect.
Matthew 5:48

The cat has vanished.

Like a ghost, he's slipped from sight.

His hiding places are vacant,

and no round eyes peek from under a

cabinet or behind a chair.

There's no telltale lump on

a freshly made bed.

How did he know it's

time to visit the vet?

Tackle the Problem

Someone once said, "Happiness is not the absence of conflict, but the ability to cope with it."

When we attempt to hide from conflict or escape from doing what we clearly need to do, negative consequences follow. We allow problems to become more serious; we leave for someone else our duties and responsibilities; we fall prey to fear, stress, or denial.

Throughout the Bible, God repeatedly assures us of His presence. Our Heavenly Father lets us know that wherever we must go, He will come along. His strength gives us the ability to cope with anything we must do.

I urge you to live a life
worthy of the calling you have received.
Ephesians 4:1 NIV

Haiku of a Hungry Cat

I want breakfast now.
Meow. Meow. Meow. MEOW. MEOW. MEOW! MEOW!!
Oh, did I wake you?

It is time for lunch!
Your e-mail can wait, or else
I chew on cables.

Hey, it's dinner time!
What do you mean, "too early"?
Open cat food. Now.

Author Unknown

From the Will of Madame Dupuis, 17th Century

If both cats should survive me, thirty sous a week must be laid out upon them, in order that they may live well. They are to be served daily, in a clean and proper manner, with two meals of meat soup, the same as we eat ourselves, but it is to be given to them separately in two soup plates. The bread is not be to cut up into the soup, but must be broken into squares the size of a nut, otherwise they will refuse to eat it. A ration of meat, finely minced, is to be added to it; the whole is then to be mildly seasoned, put into a clean pan, covered close, and carefully simmered before it is dished up.

There's not a hint of doubt on her part. The moment a lap is available, the speckled kitten hops on it and accepts her strokes as her due. She never hesitates, never wonders what she did to deserve it, but claims this comfortable human lap as her own - and it is.

Just Because

As adults, we're used to getting what we want by working for it. Our accomplishments, our successes, and our possessions come as a result of our willingness and ability to earn them.

God works differently. He has loved each of us since the beginning of time, so there's nothing for us to earn – it's ours already. He has mercy on us because He is a merciful God, so there's nothing for us to work for – it's ours already.

When it comes to God, His kindness, grace, strength, compassion, and favor are ours just because that's the kind of God He is.

Not by works of righteousness which we have done,
but according to his mercy he saved us.
Titus 3:5

Timid, skittish kitten, what have you seen in your short life? Why do you hide at the slightest sound, and why do you back away from an outstretched hand? Only the smell of food tempts you to crawl outside your shelter, and you eat quickly, watching warily all the while.

A New Season

Painful life experiences often leave heart-deep scars. Even though danger is long past, fear still lingers. It affects our present relationships and experiences, and even our perception of God.

We may never know this side of heaven why it has happened to us, but we do know that we have survived it. We also know that God has given us a new day and a new season to reach out for His blessings in joy and gratitude. Painful experiences leave scars, but they also leave strength and wisdom, giving us the opportunity to help those enduring similar trials now.

Rejoice, inasmuch as ye are partakers of Christ's sufferings; that, when his glory shall be revealed, ye may be glad also with exceeding joy.
1 Peter 4:13

I've met many thinkers and many cats,
but the wisdom of cats is infinitely superior.

Hippolyte Taine

A man has to work so hard so that something of his personality stays alive. A tomcat has it so easy, he has only to spray and his presence is there for years on rainy days.

Albert Einstein

In the overall scheme of things, it's of no real importance which way the toilet paper roll is mounted - unless, of course, you have a cat.

Author unknown

The only risk you ever run in befriending a cat is enriching yourself.

Colette

"Meow, meow, meow!"

What do you need,

little one?

Your bowl is full, and your

pillows are arranged in the

sunshine. The birds are

chirping outside the window,

and the tabby next door has

come to call.

What do you need,

little one?

Tell me, please!

Communication

"Hear the other side." St. Augustine's quote is as pertinent today as it was in his lifetime 1,600 years ago. True communication is impossible unless both sides are willing to speak... and to listen!

In the same way, true communication with God is impossible unless we are not only willing to speak to Him, but willing to listen to Him. How has He promised to communicate with us? God has given us the Bible so we can read, hear, understand, and meditate on His words to us.

We can hear the other side loud and clear when we open and read His Word.

I will meditate in thy precepts,
and have respect unto thy ways.
I will delight myself in thy statutes:
I will not forget they word.
Psalm 119:15, 16

You took a tumble, silly kitty,
and now look at you!
Even though you landed on a thick
soft rug, your pride is hurt because
you heard us laugh.
You smooth your rumpled coat,
give us a stern look, and then primly
exit the scene of the whole debacle.

Woops!

What could be worse than embarrassing ourselves in front of others? Possibly the fear of doing so. Fear of embarrassment causes us to shrink back from speaking, from acting, from reaching out, because, after all, we might stumble.

For the few times, for example, we might introduce ourselves to someone we've already met, there are infinitely more times we welcome a grateful stranger, grasp an extended hand, embrace a soul longing for recognition and acceptance.

When we've embarrassed ourselves, we can thank God for our courage and our willingness to reach out for the sake of those around us.

Be not forgetful to entertain strangers:
for thereby some have entertained angels unawares.
Hebrews 13:2

The Cat That Walked by Himself

He will kill mice, and he will be kind to babies when he is in the house, just as long as they do not pull his tail too hard. But when he has done that, and between times, and when the moon gets up and night comes, he is the Cat that walks by himself, and all places are alike to him.

Then he goes out to the Wet Wild Woods or up the Wet Wild Trees or on the Wet Wild Roofs, waving his wild tail and walking by his wild lone.

–Rudyard Kipling

What shall we call you? We've played with various names, but we haven't yet found the sound and the syllables that fit your mischievous glance, your tousled white vest, and your mottled coat. Surely, if we could speak Cat, we would ask you how you would like to be named!

All in a Name

Our Almighty God has chosen to call us disciple... friend...beloved! The name God calls us reflects His attitude toward us and describes our relationship with Him. When He speaks our name, we're reminded of His love, mercy, forgiveness, healing, and goodwill.

What's more, God tells us His name so we can know Him as He intends to be known among believers. His name is Creator and Preserver; Savior and Shepherd; Comforter and Counselor. His name tells us who He is, what He has done, and what He continues to do for us.

What's in a name? Everything!

His name shall be called Wonderful,
Counsellor, The Mighty God,
The Everlasting Father, The Prince of Peace.
Isaiah 9:6

Poor kitty! You're not feeling well, and you're stressed even more when the pill bottle is opened and a capsule prodded into your unwilling mouth. Please swallow! Now you need a quiet place to sleep, a little extra TLC, and you'll be back to playing kitty games again.

Tender Loving Care

"In sickness and in health" is the ideal way we care for one another, and it's the real and constant way God cares for us.

Despite our best intentions to follow Him, we get spiritually sick. We experience failings and set-backs, and when we do, God does not leave us to fend for ourselves. Instead, He lifts us close to Him, assures us of His mercy, and heals our wounds with the soothing balm of His forgiveness and love.

Under the care of our Great Physician, we return not as our "old" selves, but as a renewed, re-energized, and Spirit-strengthened child of God.

They that are whole have no need of the physician, but they that are sick: I came not to call the righteous, but sinners to repentance.
Mark 2:17

The Naming of Kittens

Our old cat has kittens three -
what do you think their names should be?

One is tabby with emerald eyes,
and a tail that's long and slender,
and into a temper she quickly flies
if you ever by chance offend her.
I think we shall call her this -
I think we shall call her that -
Now, don't you think that Pepperpot
is a nice name for a cat?

One is black with a frill of white,
and her feet are all white fur,
if you stroke her she carries her tail upright
and quickly begins to purr.
I think we shall call her this -
I think we shall call her that -
Now, don't you think that Sootikin
is a nice name for a cat?

One is tortoiseshell yellow and black,
with plenty of white about him;
if you tease him, at once he sets up his back,
he's a quarrelsome one, ne'er doubt him.
I think we shall call him this -
I think we shall call him that -
Now, don't you think that Scratchaway
is a nice name for a cat?

–Thomas Hood

The tuxedo cat with his neat bow tie looks up at the human lap, and then with one swift leap he lands, quickly embraced by loving arms. He circles once, twice, three times before he settles, accepts a rub of ears and throat, and pronounces his satisfaction with a long contented purr.

It Counts

Gratitude draws people together. Taking time out to give thanks to those who have blessed our lives nurtures relationships, strengthens the bonds between us, and encourages kindness and generosity.

When we express sincere thanks to God for all He has done and continues to do for us each day, similar blessings take place. Gratitude nurtures our relationship with our Heavenly Father as we recognize Him as the giver and provider of all our blessings. The Holy Spirit increases our faith and trust, and enables us to become willing givers and sharers.

Let blessings stand counted – including the gift of a grateful heart!

In every thing give thanks:
for this is the will of God in Christ Jesus concerning you.
1 Thessalonians 5:18

The soft gray cat climbs

out of her carrier,

cautiously stepping into the room,

alert in this new strange place.

No matter where you have been in the past,

sweet one, your future comes

with a promise of food, shelter, safety,

comfort, and love in this,

your forever home.

For Always

In His great love and compassion, God welcomes each of us into His presence. When we come to Him with a humble, believing heart, He opens His arms to us, comforts us in our pains and sorrows, strengthens our faith, and gives us renewed hope in His promises.

Sure, we are free to leave His presence and look for spiritual nourishment elsewhere, but why would we want to? He provides us with everything we need! Yet even if we wander back into the storm, He will not fail to call us back to Him – back to our forever home in Him.

Come unto me, all ye that labour and are heavy laden,
and I will give you rest.
Matthew 11:28

I'm a Cat

I'm only a cat,
and I stay in my place-
Up there on your chair,
on your bed or your face!
I'm only a cat,
and I don't finicky much-
I'm happy with cream
and anchovies and such!

I'm only a cat,
and we'll get along fine,
As long as you know
I'm not yours - you're all mine!

Author Unknown

Each cat claims a place in the house. The gray tabby chooses the comfort of a soft chair, and the white cat perches on top of the scratching post. The calico prefers a spacious big bed, and the tortoiseshell - where else but sprawled across a newspaper, open book, or keyboard?

Heaven

God's promise of heaven in the future makes it possible for us to live at peace today.

Many times throughout His ministry among us, Jesus said, "Do not fear." With faith in Him and strengthened by the Holy Spirit at work in us, we need not fear the troubles and trials of life, and most of all, we need not fear the end of life – death. Why? Because Jesus overcame death when He rose from the dead, and because He promised eternal life to those who believe on His name.

In life and in death, we have a place with Him!

In my Father's house are many mansions:
if it were not so, I would have told you.
I go to prepare a place for you.
John 14:2

Two cats sit side by side on the back of a chair watching the birds outside. Their heads turn in unison when a sparrow darts to the feeder, and their tails swish like matching pendulums when a puppy enters the scene and the little flock scatters to the tops of the trees.

Lifelong Friend

Sharing good times with family and friends brings incomparable joy to life. Our days are richer when we have someone to talk to about our feelings and experiences, and it's a blessing to have people around us we can rely on, come what may.

When Jesus calls us His friends, He is inviting us to regard Him as someone we can rely on, confide in, and trust. He's the Friend who shares in our joys and sorrows, who supports our godly goals and Spirit-given desires.

Though the people around us may change, we have a lifelong and life eternal friend in Him.

I have called you friends;
for all things that I have heard of my Father
I have made known unto you.
John 15:15

It is a very inconvenient habit of kittens that, whatever you say to them, they always purr.

Lewis Carroll

There is no snooze button on a cat who wants breakfast.

Author Unknown

Cat said, "I am not a friend, and I am not a servant. I am the Cat who walks by himself, and I wish to come into your Cave."

Rudyard Kipling

The cat is above all things, a dramatist.

Margaret Benson

When my cats aren't happy,
I'm not happy. Not because I care about
their mood but because I know
they're just sitting there
thinking up ways to get even.

Percy Bysshe Shelley

People who hate cats will come back
as mice in their next life.

Author Unknown

A little drowsing cat
is an image of a perfect beatitude.

Champfleury

The cat's morning opens with a stretch and a yawn, and when she deems all things as they should be, she arises and saunters into the kitchen. After breakfast has been consumed, she sets about her toilette, then settles in the morning sun for her first nap of the day.

A Purpose under Heaven

Some people set about their life's work at an early age, while for others it takes years of seeking before they find what they feel they're meant to do.

God has a purpose for everyone. Even when we cannot perceive it, our talents, abilities, and opportunities fit into His plan for us. Though what we do may seem so insignificant compared to what someone else does, our faithfulness is significant to God.

The big picture may not be clear, for we are seeing only a small part of it. We can rely on His view, however – the artist who created it.

Never be lacking in zeal,
but keep your spiritual fervor, serving the Lord.
Romans 12:11 NIV

Sometimes the cats pass by
each other with barely
a nod of acquaintance,
and other times they stop and snarl,
daring the other to move,
turn, or blink first.
But most of the time they exchange
an affable trill before each going on
about the business of the day.

Good Words

Our words come from the mouth, but they originate in the heart. When heart and mouth are at cross purposes, words come out we didn't mean to say and our tone of voice betrays our real opinions and emotions.

The Holy Spirit works to purify our hearts and set our thoughts in a positive and productive direction. He lifts our minds toward higher things, and the words we say help and encourage, gladden and delight.

When we speak, we speak easily, convincingly, and truthfully, because we are speaking from the heart – a heart filled with the goodness of God.

Let your speech be always with grace, seasoned with salt, that ye may know how ye ought to answer every man.
Colossians 4:6

The Mouse that Barked

A mother mouse and her baby were walking along when suddenly a cat lunged at them. "Bow-wow!" the mother mouse yelled, and the cat scampered away.

Mother mouse turned to her baby and said, "See? This is why it's important to learn a foreign language!"

In order to keep a true perspective of one's importance, everyone should have a dog that will worship him and a cat that will ignore him.

Author Unknown

One of the striking differences between a cat and a lie is that a cat has only nine lives.

Mark Twain

When the mouse laughs at the cat, there's a hole nearby.

Proverb

The calico cat frets at the food bowl (has it ever been empty?) and she grumbles at the dog across the street (has he ever invaded her space?). If she's moved from a lap before she's ready, she jumps down with a spit of pure indignation. Yes, she's a fretful, fussy girl.

A Clear View

Anxiety and stress go hand in hand, and they're not a friendly pair. They take their toll on our emotional and physical health, and they certainly diminish our ability to see and appreciate life's joys and pleasures.

God invites us to give over our cares to Him. In doing so, we're freed from wasting our time with unproductive worry, instead using our time to define our problems, and then devise workable plans and positive solutions.

With anxiety and stress out of the picture, we're left with a much more realistic view of our true situation.

Consider the lilies how they grow: they toil not,
they spin not; and yet I say unto you,
that Solomon in all his glory
was not arrayed like one of these.
Luke 12:27

The mottled cat

stands at her plate,

waiting for her human

to open the cupboard and

reach for a can of her food.

She watches expectantly

as her human moves around the kitchen,

but when the cupboard is ignored,

the mottled cat lets out a loud meow:

Cat food comes first.

Priorities

A glance at our daily planner... a scan of our checkbook... like nothing else, these two reveal our priorities. Where we spend our time and money tells beyond a doubt what we consider worthwhile.

When we support God's work on Earth in proportion to our income, we have proof that God is important in our lives. When we share our time with others by listening, caring, and helping according to our abilities, we have evidence that the Holy Spirit is at work in our heart.

The Spirit-inspired decision to put Him first in life makes everything else fall into its God-given place.

Seek ye first the kingdom of God, and his righteousness; and all these things shall be added unto you.
Matthew 6:33

Make Yourself at Home

A shivering scrap edges from the cat basket,
and vanishes behind the sofa.
"Poor little soul," they say,
"Perhaps a little plaice, a little milk."
"Don't startle her."

By morning she has scattered
food across the kitchen.
Established a bed in the linen basket.
Removed the vegetables from the rack.
Shredded a roll of toilet paper -

Climbed the lace curtains -
to their detriment.
Walked milk into the passage.
Used her box - with a vigorous
displacement of the litter.
And fallen asleep on the stove.

She wakes and beams
at the first person down.
"I like it here," she signals.
"How about a game of string?"

-Author Unknown

From the day he entered life until the day he died, the tom never took to his feline housemates. He growled and hissed his way to reigning cat, preserving his spot through a grand old age. Did his heart ever hunger as he watched the others frolic from his lofty throne?

Model Servant

"It's lonely at the top," as those who have risen to great heights in the world tell us. Yet we don't need to be the president of a corporation or a country to experience a similar loneliness. All we need to do is imagine ourselves better than others.

Jesus came from heaven to walk among us, and His life illustrates how He would have us regard one another. Though He could have flaunted His glory, wisdom, and power, He instead lived a life of service and sacrifice. He never looked down at the humble, but across to all with mercy, compassion, and all-encompassing love.

I am among you as he that serveth.
Luke 22:27

Sweet soul,

what happened to the

hand that used to feed you,

to the chair you loved to sleep in,

to the world you used to know?

You surely look unhappy in the

shelter, where you were taken;

yet it is in this place that a

loving heart has found you.

Forever Friends

Something clicks, and we know we've found a forever friend. It's the person we feel we've known for years, even though it's been only a few minutes. It's the one we can confide in, trust, and depend on—the one who will bless our lives in ways we can't yet imagine.

Relationships are God's way of giving us opportunities to share our interests and abilities, our presence and our caring with others. Friends inspire us and encourage us. They help us through our challenges, and they join us in our celebrations.

Thank God for friends!

Iron sharpeneth iron; so a man
sharpeneth the countenance of his friend.
Proverbs 27:17

Kitty's Bedtime Prayer

Now I lay me down to sleep,
I pray this cushy life to keep.
I pray for toys that look like mice,
and sofa cushions, soft and nice.

For grocery bags where I can hide,
just like a tiger, crouched inside!
I pray for gourmet Kitty snacks,
and someone nice to scratch my back.

For window sills all warm and bright,
for shadows to explore at night.
I pray I'll always stay real cool,
and keep the secret feline rule

To NEVER tell a human that...
the world is really ruled by CATS!

–Author Unknown

You crouch, fixing huge eyes on the wall, staring intently at – what? My faulty vision sees nothing. No moth, no gnat; no sunbeam or shadow; nothing to draw your rapt attention, your keen and silent scrutiny. Or… is it a ghost you see? Is there a ghost in here?

Solid Ground

The more we hear what others say about God, the more questions arise in our mind. What should we believe about sin, forgiveness, and salvation? Where can we learn the truth?

As we faithfully read and study the Bible, the Holy Spirit directs us to God's answers and His truth. Only by knowing what the Bible says can we protect ourselves from those who see things that aren't there, who claim things about God not in accordance with His Word.

Being grounded in scripture gives us the ability to separate truth from falsehood, God's Word from the phantoms of human imagination.

Beloved, believe not every spirit, but try the spirits whether they are of God: because many false prophets are gone out into the world.
1 John 4:1

Curtains flutter in the window,

the sounds of birdsong attend

your kitty dreams.

Your human is busy in the kitchen

fixing a plate of your favorite fish,

and a fresh cool bowl of water

awaits your tongue.

Perhaps you'll doze a little longer -

or perhaps you'll decide to eat.

It's a purrfect afternoon!

Purrfection

God created the world in six days, and on the seventh, He rested. From the beginning, God set a pattern for us to follow.

It's easy to tell ourselves we're too busy for rest and recreation. Many of us feel guilty taking time out to go for a walk, read a book, visit a museum, or spend a weekend away. When we neglect recreation, however, our effectiveness at work and our joy in life diminish.

God set the pattern, balancing work and rest, labor and relaxation. It's His recommendation for a purrfect day!

To every thing there is a season,
and a time to every purpose under the heaven.
Ecclesiastes 3:1

Bless Them All, Dear Lord

Hear our prayer, Lord, for all animals
May they be well-fed
and well-treated and happy;
Protect them from hunger
and fear and suffering.

And, we pray, protect especially, dear Lord,
The little Cat who is the companion of our home –
Keep her safe as she goes out,
And bring her back to comfort us.

Amen

The End